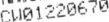

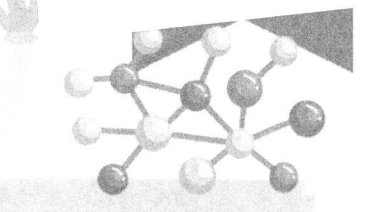

SUPER SILLY SCIENCE KNOCK KNOCK JOKES

FOR KIDS AGED 6-9

LAUGH OUT LOUD WITH HOURS OF FUN SPACE AND SCIENCE JOKES FOR SMART KIDS WHO WANT TO BUILD A SENSE OF HUMOR

COPYRIGHT GIGGLES AND GRINS 2023- ALL RIGHTS RESERVED.

THE CONTENT CONTAINED WITHIN THIS BOOK MAY NOT BE REPRODUCED, DUPLICATED OR TRANSMITTED WITHOUT DIRECT WRITTEN PERMISSION FROM THE AUTHOR OR THE PUBLISHER.

UNDER NO CIRCUMSTANCES WILL ANY BLAME OR LEGAL RESPONSIBILITY BE HELD AGAINST THE PUBLISHER, OR AUTHOR, FOR ANY DAMAGES, REPARATION, OR MONETARY LOSS DUE TO THE INFORMATION CONTAINED WITHIN THIS BOOK. EITHER DIRECTLY OR INDIRECTLY. YOU ARE RESPONSIBLE FOR YOUR OWN CHOICES, ACTIONS, AND RESULTS.

LEGAL NOTICE:

THIS BOOK IS COPYRIGHT PROTECTED. THIS BOOK IS ONLY FOR PERSONAL USE. YOU CANNOT AMEND, DISTRIBUTE, SELL, USE, QUOTE, OR PARAPHRASE ANY PART OR THE CONTENT WITHIN THIS BOOK WITHOUT THE CONSENT OF THE AUTHOR OR PUBLISHER.

DISCLAIMER NOTICE:

PLEASE NOTE THAT THE INFORMATION CONTAINED WITHIN THIS DOCUMENT IS FOR EDUCATIONAL AND ENTERTAINMENT PURPOSES ONLY. ALL EFFORT HAS BEEN EXECUTED TO PRESENT ACCURATE, UP-TO-DATE, AND RELIABLE, COMPLETE INFORMATION. NO WARRANTIES OF ANY KIND ARE DECLARED OR IMPLIED. READERS ACKNOWLEDGE THAT THE AUTHOR IS NOT ENGAGING IN THE RENDERING OF LEGAL, FINANCIAL, MEDICAL OR PROFESSIONAL ADVICE. THE CONTENT WITHIN THIS BOOK HAS BEEN DERIVED FROM VARIOUS SOURCES. PLEASE CONSULT A LICENSED PROFESSIONAL BEFORE ATTEMPTING ANY TECHNIQUES OUTLINED IN THIS BOOK.

BY READING THIS DOCUMENT, THE READER AGREES THAT UNDER NO CIRCUMSTANCES IS THE AUTHOR RESPONSIBLE FOR ANY LOSSES, DIRECT OR INDIRECT, WHICH ARE INCURRED AS A RESULT OF THE USE OF THE INFORMATION CONTAINED WITHIN THIS DOCUMENT, INCLUDING, BUT NOT LIMITED TO, – ERRORS, OMISSIONS, OR INACCURACIES.

TABLE OF CONTENT

INTRODUCTION *1*
HOW TO PLAY *2*
SPACE JOKES *3-25*
SCIENCE JOKES *26-58*
ONE LINERS *59-78*
REVIEW *79*

INTRODUCTION

WELCOME TO THE ABSURD WORLD OF KNOCK-KNOCK JOKES WITH A SCIENCE OR SPACE THEME! THIS BOOK IS JAM-PACKED WITH JOKES THAT WILL MAKE YOU LAUGH OUT LOUD AND KEEP YOU ENGAGED FOR A VERY LONG TIME.

THIS BOOK CONTAINS SOMETHING FOR EVERY YOUNG SCIENTIST AND SPACE ENTHUSIAST, FROM THE EXTRAORDINARY METEOR SHOWERS TO THE ALIENS' HYSTERICAL LAUGHING, FROM THE PLANETARY PUNS TO THE COSMIC ONE-LINERS. THESE JOKES ARE IDEAL FOR CHILDREN AGES 6 TO 9 WHO ENJOY LEARNING ABOUT THE WONDERS OF THE COSMOS AND DEVELOPING THEIR SENSE OF HUMOR IN THE PROCESS.

THERE ARE MANY ONE-LINERS AND KNOCK-KNOCK JOKES THAT ARE ABSURD, STUPID, AND OUT OF THIS WORLD. EVERYONE WILL BE CHUCKLING WHILE LEARNING ABOUT THE WONDERS OF SCIENCE AND SPACE THANKS TO THESE JOKES AND ONE-LINERS, WHICH ARE EXCELLENT FOR BUILDING RELATIONSHIPS WITH FRIENDS AND FAMILY.

PREPARE TO LAUNCH INTO A WORLD OF JOY AND LAUGHTER! THIS BOOK CONTAINS SOMETHING FOR EVERY LITTLE SPACE ADVENTURER, WHETHER YOU'RE SEEKING JOKES ABOUT ALIENS, PLANETS, OR BLACK HOLES OR JUST WANT TO APPRECIATE THE BRILLIANT ONE-LINERS. LET'S START WITH SOME INCREDIBLY CRAZY KNOCK-KNOCK JOKES WITH A SPACE AND SCIENTIFIC THEME!

HOW TO PLAY

HOW TO PLAY KNOCK KNOCK JOKES

START BY SAYING "KNOCK KNOCK" TO YOUR FRIEND OR FAMILY MEMBER. THE OTHER PERSON SHOULD THEN SAY, "WHO'S THERE?" TO PROMPT THE JOKE. NEXT, SAY A NAME OR WORD THAT SOUNDS LIKE THE START OF A JOKE, SUCH AS "BOO."
THE OTHER PERSON SHOULD THEN SAY, "BOO WHO?" TO PROMPT THE PUNCHLINE. FINALLY, DELIVER THE PUNCHLINE, WHICH SHOULD BE A FUNNY PLAY ON WORDS OR PUNS THAT ARE RELATED TO THE NAME OR WORD YOU GAVE EARLIER.

FOR EXAMPLE:

PERSON 1: KNOCK KNOCK.
PERSON 2: WHO'S THERE?
PERSON 1: BOO.
PERSON 2: BOO, WHO?
PERSON 1: DON'T CRY; IT'S JUST A JOKE!

REMEMBER, THE PUNCHLINE SHOULD ALWAYS BE SILLY AND UNEXPECTED TO MAKE IT FUN AND ENTERTAINING FOR EVERYONE. KNOCK-KNOCK JOKES ARE A GREAT WAY TO SHARE A LAUGH WITH YOUR FRIENDS AND FAMILY, AND YOU CAN COME UP WITH YOUR OWN JOKES OR FIND THEM IN JOKE BOOKS OR ONLINE.

SPACE KNOCK KNOCK

KNOCK KNOCK

WHOS THERE

ASTRONAUT!

ASTRONAUT WHO

ASTRONAUT WHO IS READY TO GO TO SPACE?

SPACE KNOCK KNOCK

KNOCK KNOCK

WHOS THERE

ROCKET

ROCKET WHO

ROCKET ABOUT TO BLAST OFF!

SPACE KNOCK KNOCK

KNOCK KNOCK

WHOS THERE

GALILEO

GALILEO WHO

GALILEO THE GUY WHO DISCOVERED JUPITORS MOONS

SPACE KNOCK KNOCK

KNOCK KNOCK

WHOS THERE

PLANET

PLANET WHO

PLANET OF APES, DO YOU WANT TO WATCH IT?

SPACE KNOCK KNOCK

KNOCK KNOCK

WHOS THERE

METEOR!

METEOR! WHO

METEOR SHOWER OR METEORITE, WHICH ONE DO YOU LIKE MORE?

SPACE KNOCK KNOCK

KNOCK KNOCK

WHOS THERE

NEPTUNE!

NEPTUNE WHO

NEPTUNE, KING OF THE SEA, DO YOU WANT TO EXPLORE SPACE WITH ME?

SPACE KNOCK KNOCK

KNOCK KNOCK

WHOS THERE

BLACK HOLE!

BLACK HOLE WHO

BLACK HOLE, NO ONE KNOWS WHAT HAPPENS INSIDE YOU!

SPACE KNOCK KNOCK

KNOCK KNOCK

WHOS THERE

SATURN!

SATURN WHO

SATURN, ALL THE PLANETS, AND LET'S EXPLORE THE UNIVERSE!

SPACE KNOCK KNOCK

KNOCK KNOCK

WHOS THERE

JUPITER!

JUPITER WHO

JUPITER HIGH, IT'S TIME TO EXPLORE THE SKY!

SPACE KNOCK KNOCK

KNOCK KNOCK

WHOS THERE

STAR

STAR WHO

STAR LIGHT, STAR BRIGHT, LET'S LEARN ABOUT SPACE TONIGHT!

SPACE KNOCK KNOCK

KNOCK KNOCK

WHOS THERE

MOON

MOON WHO

MOON-DERING WHAT'S UP THERE IN THE SKY.

SPACE KNOCK KNOCK

KNOCK KNOCK

WHOS THERE

ALIEN!

ALIEN WHO

ALIEN-TED TO MEET YOU!

SPACE KNOCK KNOCK

KNOCK KNOCK

WHOS THERE

COMET!

COMET WHO

COMET ME, BRO, LET'S EXPLORE THE COSMOS!

SPACE KNOCK KNOCK

KNOCK KNOCK

WHOS THERE

GRAVITY!

GRAVITY WHO

GRAVITY ALWAYS PULLS ME TOWARDS YOU!

SPACE KNOCK KNOCK

KNOCK KNOCK

WHOS THERE

MARTIAN!

MARTIAN WHO

MARTIAN THIS WAY TO THE ROCKET, LET'S GO!

SPACE KNOCK KNOCK

KNOCK KNOCK

WHOS THERE

TELESCOPE!

TELESCOPE WHO

TELESCOPE YOU A SECRET – I LOVE LOOKING AT THE STARS AT NIGHT!

SPACE KNOCK KNOCK

KNOCK KNOCK

WHOS THERE

ORBIT!

ORBIT WHO

ORBIT AROUND THE SUN, LET'S HAVE SOME FUN!

SPACE KNOCK KNOCK

KNOCK KNOCK

WHOS THERE

INTERRUPTING ASTEROID

INTERRUPTING ASTEROID WHO

SORRY, I CAN'T HEAR YOU OVER THE SOUND OF MY IMPACT!

SPACE KNOCK KNOCK

KNOCK KNOCK

WHOS THERE

MOON

MOON WHO

MOON-DERFUL TO SEE YOU!

SPACE KNOCK KNOCK

KNOCK KNOCK

WHOS THERE

VENUS

VENUS WHO

VENUS EARTHS NEXT DOOR NEIGHBOR

SPACE KNOCK KNOCK

KNOCK KNOCK

WHOS THERE

MARS

MARS WHO

MARS BARS ARE OUT OF THIS WORLD!

SPACE KNOCK KNOCK

KNOCK KNOCK

WHOS THERE

MERCURY

MERCURY WHO

MER-CURY AND NANN BREAD PLEASE!

SPACE KNOCK KNOCK

KNOCK KNOCK

WHOS THERE

PLUTO

PLUTO WHO

PLUTO IS NO LONGER A PLANET, BUT IT'S STILL OUT THERE!

SCIENCE KNOCK KNOCK

KNOCK KNOCK

WHOS THERE

BOHR

BOHR WHO

BOHR-ING SCIENCE CLASS, BUT I'M LEARNING A LOT!

SCIENCE KNOCK KNOCK

KNOCK KNOCK

WHOS THERE

BEAKER

BEAKER WHO

BEAKER WE CAN DO SOME COOL EXPERIMENTS IN SCIENCE CLASS TODAY!

SCIENCE KNOCK KNOCK

KNOCK KNOCK

WHOS THERE

NOBEL

NOBEL WHO

NO BELL, THAT'S WHY I KNOCKED!

SCIENCE KNOCK KNOCK

KNOCK KNOCK

WHOS THERE

MOLECULE

MOLECULE WHO

MOLECULE YOU LATER, AFTER I FINISH THIS EXPERIMENT!

SCIENCE KNOCK KNOCK

KNOCK KNOCK

WHOS THERE

NEWTON

NEWTON WHO

NEWTON, I WAS JUST PLAYING CHAP DOOR RUN AWAY

SCIENCE KNOCK KNOCK

KNOCK KNOCK

WHOS THERE

EINSTEIN

EINSTEIN WHO

EINSTEINS A GREAT SCIENTIST, JUST LIKE YOU!

SCIENCE KNOCK KNOCK

KNOCK KNOCK

WHOS THERE

BUNSEN

BUNSEN WHO

BUNSEN BURNER, LET'S HEAT UP SOME EXPERIMENTS!

SCIENCE KNOCK KNOCK

KNOCK KNOCK

WHOS THERE

ELEMENT

ELEMENT WHO

ELEMENT OF SURPRISE, SCIENCE CAN BE SO FUN!

SCIENCE KNOCK KNOCK

> KNOCK KNOCK

WHOS THERE

> LAB

LAB WHO

> LAB-RATORY EXPERIMENTS ARE SO MUCH FUN!

SCIENCE KNOCK KNOCK

KNOCK KNOCK

WHOS THERE

VOLCANO

VOLCANO WHO

VOLCANO, I THINK WE'RE GOING TO ERUPT WITH EXCITEMENT ABOUT SCIENCE!

SCIENCE KNOCK KNOCK

KNOCK KNOCK

WHOS THERE

FOSSIL

FOSSIL WHO

FOSSIL-LY, LET'S LEARN ABOUT THE HISTORY OF THE EARTH!

SCIENCE KNOCK KNOCK

KNOCK KNOCK

WHOS THERE

ATOM

ATOM WHO

ATOM-IC SCIENCE EXPERIMENTS ARE SO COOL!

SCIENCE KNOCK KNOCK

KNOCK KNOCK

WHOS THERE

PERIODIC

PERIODIC WHO

PERIODIC TABLES ARE MY FAVORITE THING TO STUDY IN SCIENCE!

SCIENCE KNOCK KNOCK

KNOCK KNOCK

WHOS THERE

CHEMIST

CHEMIST WHO

CHEMIST-RY, LET'S MIX THINGS UP AND SEE WHAT WE CAN CREATE!

SCIENCE KNOCK KNOCK

> KNOCK KNOCK

WHOS THERE

> BACTERIA

BACTERIA WHO

> BACTERIA GOOD OR BAD, LET'S LEARN ABOUT THEM ALL!

SCIENCE KNOCK KNOCK

KNOCK KNOCK

WHOS THERE

ECOLOGY

ECOLOGY WHO

ECOLOGY-TED TO LEARN ABOUT THE ENVIRONMENT AND HOW WE CAN PROTECT IT!

SCIENCE KNOCK KNOCK

KNOCK KNOCK

WHOS THERE

ELECTRON

ELECTRON WHO

ELECTRON-TIC SCIENCE EXPERIMENTS ARE SO FASCINATING!

SCIENCE KNOCK KNOCK

KNOCK KNOCK

WHOS THERE

GEOLOGIST

GEOLOGIST WHO

GEOLOGIST-ICALLY SPEAKING, STUDYING ROCKS IS SO INTERESTING!

SCIENCE KNOCK KNOCK

KNOCK KNOCK

WHOS THERE

MARSUPIAL

MARSUPIAL WHO

MARSUPIAL-LY INTERESTED IN BIOLOGY AND THE STUDY OF ANIMALS!

SCIENCE KNOCK KNOCK

> KNOCK KNOCK

WHOS THERE

> HYDROLOGY

HYDROLOGY WHO

> HYDROLOGY IS THE STUDY OF WATER, AND IT'S SO IMPORTANT TO OUR PLANET!

SCIENCE KNOCK KNOCK

KNOCK KNOCK

WHOS THERE

INERTIA

INERTIA WHO

INERTIA, NOTHING CAN STOP US FROM LEARNING ABOUT SCIENCE!

SCIENCE KNOCK KNOCK

KNOCK KNOCK

WHOS THERE

NEURON

NEURON WHO

NEURON TO LEARN ABOUT THE BRAIN AND NERVOUS SYSTEM!

SCIENCE KNOCK KNOCK

KNOCK KNOCK

WHOS THERE

ROBOT

ROBOT WHO

ROBOT ANY GOOD SCIENCE BOOKS LATELY?

SCIENCE KNOCK KNOCK

KNOCK KNOCK

WHOS THERE

DNA

DNA WHO

DNA, IT'S AMAZING WHAT CAN BE DISCOVERED ABOUT OURSELVES THROUGH GENETICS!

SCIENCE KNOCK KNOCK

KNOCK KNOCK

WHOS THERE

ZOOLOGY

ZOOLOGY WHO

ZOOLOGY IS THE STUDY OF ANIMALS, LET'S DISCOVER SOME NEW SPECIES!

SCIENCE KNOCK KNOCK

KNOCK KNOCK

WHOS THERE

MAGNET

MAGNET WHO

MAGNET-IC SCIENCE EXPERIMENTS ARE SO MUCH FUN!

SCIENCE KNOCK KNOCK

KNOCK KNOCK

WHOS THERE

PLUTO

PLUTO WHO

PLUTO-NIUM IS A FASCINATING ELEMENT!

SCIENCE KNOCK KNOCK

KNOCK KNOCK

WHOS THERE

SOLAR

SOLAR WHO

SOLAR SYSTEM, HERE WE COME!

SCIENCE KNOCK KNOCK

KNOCK KNOCK

WHOS THERE

GENIE

GENIE WHO

GENIE-ETICS IS A COOL SCIENCE SUBJECT!

SCIENCE KNOCK KNOCK

> KNOCK KNOCK

WHOS THERE

> LIGHT

LIGHT WHO

> LIGHT UP YOUR MIND WITH SCIENCE

SCIENCE KNOCK KNOCK

> KNOCK KNOCK

WHOS THERE

> CELL

CELL WHO

> CELL-EBRATE SCIENCE

SCIENCE KNOCK KNOCK

KNOCK KNOCK

WHOS THERE

SCIENCE

SCIENCE WHO

SCIENCE-TIFIC DISCOVERIES ARE WAITING TO BE MADE!

SCIENCE KNOCK KNOCK

KNOCK KNOCK

WHOS THERE

ZINC

ZINC WHO

ZINC YOUR MIND INTO SCIENCE

SILLY ONE LINERS

WHY DID THE MARTIAN REFUSE A SECOND SERVING OF POTATOES?

HE WAS ALREADY STUFFED WITH STARS.

HOW DO YOU SORT OUT A SPACE PARTY?

YOU PLANET!

SILLY ONE LINERS

WHY DON'T SCIENTISTS TRUST ATOMS?

BECAUSE THEY MAKE UP EVERYTHING

LOL HA

WHY DID THE COMET GO TO THE DENTIST?

IT HAD A MASSIVE CRATER

SILLY ONE LINERS

WHY WAS THE MATH BOOK SAD?

IT HAD TOO MANY PROBLEMS.

LOL HA

HOW DOES THE SUN CUT ITS HAIR?

ECLIPSE IT!

SILLY ONE LINERS

WHAT DO PLANETS LIKE TO READ?

COMET BOOKS

LOL HA

HOW DOES THE MOON STAY COOL?

IT USES A LUNAR FAN

SILLY ONE LINERS

WHAT'S AN ASTRONAUT'S FAVORITE MEAL?

LAUNCH

WHY DID THE SCIENTIST INSTALL A KNOCKER ON HIS DOOR?

HE WANTED TO WIN THE NOBEL PRIZE

SILLY ONE LINERS

WHY WAS THE TELESCOPE FEELING SAD?

IT WASN'T SEEING ANY STARS

LOL   HA

WHAT DOES A SCIENTIST WEAR TO A PARTY?

A LAB COAT

SILLY ONE LINERS

WHY DID THE DINOSAUR GO TO THE SPACE MUSEUM?

TO LEARN ABOUT HIS EXTINCT RELATIVES

LOL HA

HOW DOES THE SUN SAY GOODBYE TO ITS CHILDREN?

"SEE YOU NEXT LIGHT!"

SILLY ONE LINERS

WHY DID THE ASTRONAUT CROSS THE ROAD

TO GRAB A MILKY WAY BAR

HOW DO YOU KNOW WHEN THE MOON HAS HAD ENOUGH TO EAT?

WHEN ITS FULL

SILLY ONE LINERS

WHAT'S AN ALIEN'S FAVORITE KEY ON A COMPUTER KEYBOARD?

THE SPACE BAR

LOL HA

HOW DOES A SCIENTIST FRESHEN THEIR BREATH?

WITH EXPERI-MINTS!

SILLY ONE LINERS

HOW DOES A SCIENTIST KEEP THEIR HAIR IN PLACE?

WITH EXPERI-GEL!

WHY DID THE PLANT BREAK UP WITH THE SUN?

BECAUSE IT NEEDED A LITTLE SPACE TO GROW

SILLY ONE LINERS

WHAT DID THE DNA SAY TO THE OTHER DNA?

"DO THESE GENES MAKE ME LOOK BIG?"

WHAT DO YOU CALL AN ALLIGATOR IN A LAB COAT?

AN INVESTIGATOR!

SILLY ONE LINERS

WHY DID THE DINOSAUR REFUSE TO RIDE THE SPACESHIP?

IT WANTED TO STAY GROUNDED

LOL HA

WHAT DO YOU GET WHEN YOU CROSS A SPACE SHUTTLE WITH A HEDGEHOG?

SONIC BOOM!

SILLY ONE LINERS

WHY DID THE GRAPE STOP IN THE MIDDLE OF THE EXPERIMENT?

IT RAN OUT OF JUICE!

WHY DID THE CHICKEN JOIN NASA?

TO BECOME AN EGG-STRONAUT!

SILLY ONE LINERS

WHY DID THE PROTON CROSS THE ROAD?

TO GET TO THE POSITIVE SIDE!

LOL HA

WHY DID THE ATOM GO TO THE GYM?

TO GAIN SOME ATOMIC MASS!

SILLY ONE LINERS

WHAT DID THE MOON SAY TO THE ASTRONAUT?

"I'M YOUR BIGGEST FAN!"

LOL HA

WHAT DO YOU CALL A GROUP OF ALIEN MUSICIANS?

AN EXTRA-TERRESTRIAL BAND!

SILLY ONE LINERS

WHAT DO YOU CALL A SPACESHIP THAT'S MADE OF WOOD?

THE USS SPLINTERPRISE!

WHY COULDN'T JUPITER SLEEP?

IT WAS FULL OF GAS

SILLY ONE LINERS

WHY DID THE ASTRONAUT BECOME A BEEKEEPER?

HE WANTED TO BUILD A ROCKET HIVE!

LOL HA

WHAT DID THE EARTH SAY TO THE MOON?

"YOU'RE MY BEST ORBIT!"

SILLY ONE LINERS

WHAT DID THE EARTH SAY TO THE SUN?

YOU LIGHT UP MY WORLD!

WHAT DID THE NEUTRON SAY TO THE ELECTRON?

"YOU'RE A NEGATIVE INFLUENCE!"

SILLY ONE LINERS

WHAT DID THE SUN SAY WHEN IT FELL IN LOVE WITH THE MOON?

I'M OVER THE MOON IN LOVE

WHAT DID THE ASTRONAUT SAY WHEN HE GOT LOST IN SPACE?

"I NEED TO PLANET BETTER!"

SILLY ONE LINERS

WHAT DID ONE ATOM SAY TO THE OTHER?

"I THINK I LOST AN ELECTRON!" THE OTHER ATOM ASKED, "ARE YOU POSITIVE?"

WHY DID THE SKELETON GO TO THE LAB?

TO HAVE A BONE DENSITY TEST!

REVIEW

THANK YOU SO MUCH FOR CHOOSING TO READ OUR SUPER SILLY SPACE AND SCIENCE KNOCK KNOCK JOKES FOR KIDS BOOK! WE HOPE YOUR LITTLE ONE HAD A BLAST READING AND LAUGHING AT OUR SPACE, SCIENCE-THEMED JOKES, AND ONE-LINERS.

IF YOU AND YOUR FAMILY ENJOYED THE BOOK, WE'D BE OVER THE "MOON" IF YOU COULD TAKE A FEW MOMENTS TO LEAVE A REVIEW ON THE RETAILER'S WEBSITE WHERE YOU PURCHASED IT FROM. YOUR FEEDBACK IS INCREDIBLY VALUABLE TO US AND HELPS US REACH MORE FAMILIES WHO MIGHT ALSO ENJOY OUR BOOK.

REVIEWS ALSO HELP OTHER FAMILIES DECIDE WHETHER OUR BOOK IS RIGHT FOR THEM, SO YOUR THOUGHTS AND OPINIONS CAN MAKE A BIG DIFFERENCE. WE WOULD LOVE TO HEAR WHAT YOU AND YOUR KIDS THOUGHT OF OUR JOKES AND ONE-LINERS.

WE HAD A BLAST CREATING THIS BOOK AND HOPE YOUR FAMILY HAD JUST AS MUCH FUN READING IT. THANK YOU FOR CHOOSING OUR BOOK AND FOR SHARING IN OUR LOVE FOR ALL THINGS SPACE AND SCIENCE!

BEST REGARDS,
GIGGLES AND GRINS

Printed in Great Britain
by Amazon